DON'T PICK ON ME

How To Handle Bullying

DON'T PICK ON ME

HOW TO HANDLE BULLYING

ROSEMARY STONES

Illustrated by Belinda Evans

Piccadilly Press · London

For Melanie Hart

Text Copyright © Rosemary Stones, 1993
Illustration copyright © Belinda Evans, 1993
Reprinted 1993

Phototypeset by Spooner Graphics, London NW5
Printed and bound by Bell & Bain Ltd, Glasgow
for the publishers, Piccadilly Press Ltd.,
5 Castle Road, London NW1 8PR

A catalogue record for this book is available from the British Library

ISBN 1-85340-149-8 (hardback)
1-85340-159-5 (paperback)

Rosemary Stones lives in south London. She is an editor in a
publishing house. Her books for Piccadilly Press include the highly
successful sex education book, *Loving Encounters.*

Belinda Evans graduated from Hull College of Art and Design. As
well as illustrating many books, she has a stall in an arts and crafts
market where she sells hand-drawn T shirts.

Contents

Chapter One

WHAT IS BULLYING?

Chapter One

WHAT IS BULLYING?

Bullying is a way of being cruel to another person. It can involve:

* calling someone names
* making fun of someone in a nasty way
* stealing or breaking someone's things
* pushing someone or hitting them
* frightening someone into doing things they don't want to do

These are just some examples. Unfortunately, bullies know lots more horrible ways to bully apart from these.

Sometimes it will be very obvious to you that bullying is going on as it was to Sophie when she was being bullied:

As Sophie walked out of the school gates, Robert and Matthew grabbed her school bag, emptied her things out onto the pavement and then stamped on them and kicked them around. "We'll do this again tomorrow unless you give us your dinner money,"

3

said Matthew, "and if you tell anyone, you'll be
very sorry."

But sometimes the person doing the bullying is someone
who cares about you and wants to help you. This kind of
bullying is often disguised as "helpful" advice or criticism
so it's confusing and hard to recognise. This is what
happened to Mala:

Mala's family has just moved to a smart new
neighbourhood and Mala is missing her friends.
"What are you moping about?" her dad asks her.
"You look like a wet weekend." "I miss Laura and
Margaret", Mala tells him. "You're such an ungrateful
girl", fumes Dad, "I spend all this money so that you
can move to this beautiful house and all you do is
droop about looking miserable because you can't see
those two no-hopers."

Perhaps Mala does feel pleased and excited to be in a
smart new house but she also feels sad that she can no
longer see Laura and Margaret. Dad cannot cope with
the idea that Mala can feel sadness and loss as well as
excitement and pleasure so he tries to make her feel that
her feelings of sadness and loss are not important. Dad
doesn't realise that this is a kind of bullying. If Mala
allows Dad to bully her in this way, next time she feels
sad about something that is important to her, she may try
to bury that feeling rather than recognise and accept it.

Broadly speaking, there are three kinds of bullying:

1. Physical Bullying

Physical bullying is when a bully attacks someone physically by, say, pulling their hair or spitting at them or punching them.

Michael isn't good at football. He's small for his age and he finds it hard to control the ball. He always gets picked last for the team. The other boys make fun of him, banging into him "accidentally" and tripping him up when the games teacher isn't looking. Michael's mum wonders why he's always covered with bruises, but Michael won't say.

2. Verbal Bullying

Verbal means using words. Verbal bullying is when a bully hurts or frightens someone by, say, calling them names or threatening them or making them look silly.

Jane's class think that wearing the "right" label clothing is very important, from trainers to T-shirts. Jane's mum knows how important it is to Jane to have the "right" label so that she can be dressed like everyone else but these label clothes are just too expensive. Jane's classmates start to make fun of her:

5

Don't Pick on Me

"What a fleabag!" "Where did you get that coat? The Oxfam shop?" Jane wishes she didn't have to go to school; she is beginning to dread each new day.

Some adults think that verbal bullying is not important because they can't see any damage. If a bully hit you and made your nose bleed, they would find that hurt easy to understand. But if you tell them that a bully called you a stinking fleabag, they just laugh and tell you not to be so sensitive or "such a baby".

Of course words are used a lot when people are teased and it's important not to be over-sensitive about teasing (see section on teasing in this book) but verbal bullying is not the same as teasing. When people are teased any hurt is mild and no one person is ever teased all the time — everyone gets their turn to tease. Verbal bullying is both cruel and one-sided.

There is an old saying:

> Sticks and stones may break my bones
> But names can never hurt me.

This is not true.

Name calling and other kinds of verbal bullying can hurt very much indeed and adults should take them seriously. One girl who was bullied physically and verbally said, "Physical hurts heal much more quickly than being called names."

3. Bullying Yourself

"People don't bully themselves!" you're probably saying. But lots of people do just that although they are often not aware that what they are doing to themselves is a kind of bullying.

This is what happened to Tabitha:

Tabitha arranged to go swimming on Saturday with

*her friend Jane. She got to the baths on time but
Jane didn't show up. After a while, Tabitha began to
say to herself: "Jane probably hasn't come because
she doesn't really like me. I expect she thinks I'm
awful. She probably doesn't want anyone from school
to see us together." (In fact, Jane had missed the bus.
She turned up full of apologies for being late.)*

This kind of inside bullying is horrible and very painful to
bear. Why should Tabitha have to put up with the
disappointment of Jane not being there as arranged *and*
have to bully herself by thinking that it's because she,
Tabitha, has something wrong with her?

How Does Bullying Work?

Bullies are people who need to hurt, threaten, frighten or
control other people.

Child bullies often get away with bullying because they
are careful to hide what they are doing from adults who
would stop them. They also rely on the people they bully
and on other children who know what is going on to
remain silent about it.

Bullies like to pick on:

* people who lack confidence and find it hard to make
friends. These are usually people who don't look
confident and happy.

8

* people who are smaller, weaker or younger than they are.

* new pupils. People who change schools and people who transfer from primary to secondary school are often at risk of bullying.

* people who are clumsy or bad at sports. These are the people who always get picked last for the team.

* people whose bodies are beginning, due to puberty, to change and develop into adult bodies. Or people who are "late developers" and whose bodies haven't yet begun to change and develop. It's easy for bullies to make people feel self-conscious or "abnormal" at this point in their lives.

* people who wear glasses; have a stammer; wear braces; have a hearing aid; have big ears or are in some other way different.

* people who have different skin colour; cultural background; regional accent; religion or class.

* people who appear to be well off with lots of possessions, or, at the other extreme, people who appear to be badly off with few possessions.

* people who are in the wrong place at the wrong time. For example, the unlucky person who finds her/himself alone in the toilets when the bullies walk in.

* people whose parents are a focus of public attention — perhaps their dad is in prison or their mum is a member of parliament.

Of course, if any of these apply to you, you won't necessarily be bullied. Perhaps you're good at sticking up for yourself; perhaps your school has a good atmosphere and everyone accepts and is happy about the fact that not everyone is the same; perhaps your school has an anti-bullying policy.

The Impact of Bullying

The impact of bullying can be very serious indeed. One sixteen-year-old girl, Katharine Bamber, killed herself as a result of being bullied at school. In her suicide note, she told her parents that she could no longer bear her classmates' mockery and taunts. Sadly, she is not the only young person to have committed suicide because of bullying. Other recent cases include twelve-year-old Stephen Woodhall who hung himself after being picked on by fourteen- and fifteen-year-old boys who stole his lunch money and called his dad names and thirteen-year-old Kelly Farrar who died after taking a lethal mixture of pills. She had been warned by school bullies that she would be picked on the next day.

Sir Ranulph Fiennes, the explorer, describes in his autobiography how he was bullied at his private school. Crying hopelessly in his bed at nights, he thought about killing himself by jumping off a bridge into the Thames. Fortunately, he did manage to tell his mother about what was happening to him.

Other children who have been bullied have run away from home, refused to go to school any more or have

11

become seriously depressed.

Bullying can cause so much pain and distress that some people who have been bullied are affected by it for the rest of their lives — not surprisingly, they find it hard to trust anyone ever again and they have difficulty making friends and forming relationships. People who bully risk getting into the habit of using aggression and violence to get their own way and never learning to treat themselves and others well.

AN ATMOSPHERE OF FEAR

Apart from the hurt suffered by people who are actually being bullied, the fact that bullying is going on can affect everyone else because bullying creates an atmosphere of fear:

* Even if you are not the person being bullied, it is hard to feel relaxed and happy when you know that someone else is being hurt. You also wonder if it's going to be your turn next.

* It's hard to have confidence in the teachers or other adults around if they either don't notice what's going on, or notice but don't do anything to stop it.

* If the bullies are the adults, you can feel quite despairing. You need to tell an adult you can trust about what is happening.

* If your friends are being bullied, you might be frightened to be seen talking to them in the playground. At the same time, you'll probably feel ashamed of yourself for not sticking up for them. This is a heavy burden to carry.

* If bullying takes place in the toilets, you will have to plan to go when the bullies are not around. Not very convenient!

* If bullies hang round the school gate at home time, you might have to wait for your friends every day so that you can all leave safely together.

While keeping safe tactics like these are sensible, it's just not right that you have to tiptoe around carefully all the time in order to keep the bullies at bay. It's also not right that bullies can frighten you enough to stop you sticking up for your friends. Why should the bullies get away with it?

Who Are the Bullies?

Some people bully because they just don't know any good ways of getting on with other people. Perhaps their parents fight when they have disagreements instead of discussing them and working them out. With adults like

13

that around, it's not surprising that it's difficult for a child to learn how to get on with others without fighting and bullying.

Some people bully because they are angry and upset about something and they take it out on someone else. Hurting someone else may help them to feel less hurt. This is painful for the person who is being picked on and it is also painful for the bully not to be able to cope with difficult feelings in a better way.

Some people bully because they are jealous or because they lack self confidence. If they can control other people by bullying them, this helps them to feel more powerful, confident and secure. They need to learn better ways to feel powerful and confident that don't involve frightening and hurting other people.

People who bully aren't much fun to have around. They can be described as:

aggressive   mean   insensitive   cruel   bullying

* Bullies think that getting their own way by being hurtful, aggressive or frightening is OK.

* Bullies are often thought of as stupid people who only manage to get what they want by picking on those smaller than themselves. This is not always the case.

* Some bullies are very clever people who terrorise others by making fun of them, jeering at them and manipulating them.

14

* Some bullies are very clever at pretending to be friends, gaining your confidence and then spreading malicious stories about you.

* Bullies can be found in every kind of school, from nursery to secondary, from state to private school.

* Both boys and girls can be bullies.

* Bullies sometimes bully people who are younger than they are but many also bully people their own age or older.

* Girl bullies usually prefer to use verbal bullying (cruel jokes for example) rather than physical bullying; but not always. Girl bullies also like to isolate their victim from the rest of the group and make other people ignore them. They might try to exclude them from playground games, for example.

* Boy bullies tend to rely on physical bullying or on threats; but not always.

* Some bullies like to organise themselves into groups and plan attacks on victims.

* Some bullies use threats or force to make people give them money, sweets or other items that they want. This is called extortion (forcing someone to give you something against their will).

* Some bullies are themselves the victim of bullying, sometimes by their parents or by older brothers or sisters. In turn, they then bully people of their own age or younger.

* Some adults, teachers for example, are bullies. They

use their authority to make cruel personal remarks ("Isn't it time you lost some weight, lad?"), unfair comparisons ("It's clear that your sister inherited the brains, not you."), threats and (rarely but it does happen) physical assaults.

> It is illegal for teachers in state schools to use corporal punishment (hitting, smacking or physical assault of any kind). If you go to a private school, your parents should notify the school that in no circumstances do they allow your teachers to assault you physically.

Who Are the People Who Are Bullied?

People who are bullied do not know how to defend themselves from being trampled on by other people. Sometimes they even trample on themselves by allowing a bullying and criticising voice inside themselves to attack them.

People who are bullied are often pleasant, thoughtful and friendly but they can also be described as:

**shy   timid   afraid   unassertive
lacking in confidence**

People who are bullied allow others to control them.

What Can Be Done?

Whether you are a bully or someone who is bullied, you would probably prefer to be able to describe yourself as a happy person — someone who is:

friendly   caring   fun to be with   lively
thoughtful   confident   assertive   courageous
gentle   determined

It is painful to need to be a bully. It is painful to be bullied.

Things don't have to go on being like this for you, whether you are a bully or someone who is bullied.

It is possible to find a different, happy way to be with people and to get along with people. Reading this book can be the start of your search to find this different, happy way.

Chapter Two

STICKING UP FOR YOURSELF!

Chapter Two

STICKING UP FOR YOURSELF!

Niti's class is in the middle of a spelling test when the boy sitting next to her, Jason, asks in a whisper how to spell "acknowledge". Their teacher, Mr Greenacre, does not allow people to help each other in tests so Niti just shakes her head at Jason. Suddenly Mr Greenacre shouts out, "Niti! I saw you helping Jason. No marks at all for you." Niti tries to explain that she didn't say anything but Mr Greenacre won't listen. Jason doesn't say a word. After the class, Niti talks to her friend, Sonia, about it. "It's really unfair," says Sonia, "you weren't breaking any rules. You should have stuck up for yourself!"

When Mark gets to school, he sees Peter in tears - Peter's cat died that morning. This reminds Mark of how he felt when his dad had his pet rabbit put down because they weren't allowed to keep pets any more by the landlord. To shut out these painful feelings, Mark starts making fun of Peter: "What a crybaby! Did diddums' catty-watty kick the bucket, then?"

Don't Pick on Me

Mark doesn't know that it's OK to feel upset and angry about the dreadful thing that happened to his rabbit; he needs to stick up for himself by finding a better way of dealing with these feelings, a way that doesn't hurt someone else.

Both Niti and Mark need to stick up for themselves. So, how do you learn to stick up for yourself?

What is Sticking Up for Yourself?

If you want to stop being bullied
If you want to stop being a bully

you need help from someone who will always be on your side; someone you can rely on; that "someone" is you.

No one knows better than Niti and Mark that what happened wasn't their fault:

Niti didn't break the class rule.
Mark didn't deserve to have his rabbit destroyed and his grief at losing his pet ignored.

Niti and Mark can begin to stick up for themselves by keeping this in mind when the adults either won't listen or won't understand how difficult and painful the situation is.

Of course, this is just the beginning. Niti and Mark

may want to stick up for themselves by speaking up for themselves. Speaking up for yourself can be a hard thing to do if you aren't confident about your own good qualities and your own strength. After all, how will you feel if you speak up for yourself and it doesn't work? Perhaps Mr Greenacre will still refuse to listen; Mark's dad may tell him not to be such a baby about the rabbit. Things won't always go your way however unfair it is that they don't.

When this happens, what you need is to feel secure and confident inside yourself that you like yourself and that you understand how things really are. Even if Mr Greenacre won't listen or won't believe her, Niti knows that she didn't break a rule and that what happened wasn't fair. Even if Mark's dad doesn't understand how Mark feels about his rabbit, Mark knows how precious his pet was to him, how cruel it was that it had to be put down and how angry and upset he is about it. Like Niti and Mark, you will often need to be your own good friend on whom you can rely to understand how things really are for you even if no one else does.

Learning to stick up for yourself isn't something that happens overnight. Any kind of change in the way you think about yourself and in the way you behave takes time. So, stick with it.

Learning to Feel Secure and Confident Inside Yourself

To feel good about yourself inside doesn't mean that you have to be:

* physically stronger than everyone else
* cleverer than everyone else
* the same as everyone else
* richer than everyone else
* able to make people do what you want.

The kind of power that feeling good about yourself gives you is personal to you. It doesn't depend on comparisons with other people.

This is the inner power that will begin to grow and eventually enable you to stick up for yourself when other people try to bully you. If you find yourself wanting to bully someone else, your inner power will help you find a better way of coping with difficult feelings.

Inner power can become part of you and stay with you all your life. And it will keep on coming in handy.
Bullying is something that adults do to each other too!

To develop inner power, you will need to:

* understand your feelings
* be responsible for your feelings
* be responsible for your behaviour
* use your inner power.

Understanding Your Feelings

Excitement Anger Rage Depression Curiosity Terror Joy Pleasure Fear Anxiety Humiliation Surprise Contempt Enjoyment Shame Fury Boredom Loneliness Aggression Astonishment Jealousy Frustration Delight Impatience Pain Tension Irritation Friendship Selfishness Affection Restlessness

These words describe feelings that we all have. (You'll be able to think of more not listed here.)

WHAT ARE FEELINGS FOR?
Your feelings tell you what is going on inside you. It's quite normal to have feelings and it's quite normal to have all of them or some of them at different times.

ARE SOME FEELINGS BAD?
Feelings aren't "good" or "bad" — feelings just are.

Quite a lot of people are confused about this — they imagine that if you feel rage with someone you might actually harm that person or if you are jealous of someone, you might actually do them down in some way. This is not so - feelings cannot hurt anyone.

People choose whether or not their feelings lead to actions and whether these actions are good or bad:

Annette feels angry because John has borrowed her bike without asking. She chooses to hit him and pull his hair.

Sam feels angry because Joe spilt water all over his painting. He chooses to tell him how angry he feels that his work has been spoilt.

Winston feels angry because Paulette is making fun of him. He chooses not to show how angry he is.

ANGER
Anger is the feeling that most frightens people so they often pretend to themselves that they don't feel any. They think anger is a "bad" feeling to have. In fact, anger is an important feeling that should be listened to — anger tells you lots of useful things about yourself.

1. Anger tells you:
How you want to be treated (because not being well treated makes you feel angry...)

This is what happened to Jenifer:

Jenifer had a bad day at school. Her teacher told her he "hadn't got round" to looking at the story that she'd spent such a lot of time on when he'd promised to talk to her about it that day. He then told her to clear up a mess she didn't make. That evening Jenifer told her mum about it: "I feel like killing Mr Thomas!" she said crossly. "Jenifer!" said Mum, "What an awful thing to say. I won't have violent feelings and especially not from a girl."

Quite rightly, Jenifer feels angry because she wasn't well treated at school by Mr Thomas. She wants to let her mum know how cross and disappointed she feels, but mum is someone who is frightened of hearing about angry feelings. Instead of being able to talk about them with Jenifer, she tells her off for having such feelings.

Jenifer's mother is confusing Jenifer's angry feelings (which don't hurt anyone) with possible violent actions — but Jenifer is not actually planning to kill Mr Thomas.

If Jenifer goes along with her mother, she'll have to start pretending to herself that she never has feelings of anger or rage. Then she won't be able to hear the important things that these feelings are telling her.

Mum also seems to think that it's OK for boys to have angry feelings but not girls.

In fact, both girls and boys have angry, aggressive feelings (and, of course, both girls and boys have tender, caring feelings).

Unfortunately some parents (like Jenifer's mum) find it hard to accept and think about their own difficult feelings let alone their children's. They can't think about such feelings as anger, aggression and rage with you and try to help you to understand them because it's something they have not managed for themselves. This can be very disappointing and frustrating for you when you need someone helpful to talk to. If this happens to you, keep trying to find a trustworthy adult or older person who is good at talking and thinking about feelings. They do exist!

2. Anger tells you:
what you think is fair (because unfairness makes you feel angry ...)

This is what happened to Gabrielle:

Gabrielle and Bernadette are expected to take turns washing up but Gabrielle often gets out of her turn because she "can't be late for Guides". Today, Bernadette has been invited to a friend's to see a video but when she asks to leave early mum refuses to let her. "You can watch videos any old time," she says. Gabrielle feels angry — why can't Mum understand that being invited to see the video is important to her? It's also not fair that Gabrielle gets out of the washing up so easily.

3. Anger tells you:
what you find important (because when things that are important to you are laughed at or ignored you feel angry ...)

This is what happened to Rupert:

Rupert enjoys pop music but his parents and his brother only approve of classical music. If they find him listening to pop music, they say "You can't really be enjoying that awful noise" or "Only stupid people like that kind of music."

Don't Pick on Me

Perhaps Rupert's family think they are just teasing him, but their rudeness and lack of respect for the things that Rupert enjoys is making it very hard for Rupert to stick up for himself and stay in touch with his feelings of enjoyment about pop music. He feels angry that his family are so dismissive about his preferences - after all, he doesn't make rude remarks about their musical taste.

YOUR FEELINGS BELONG TO YOU

Some people like to tell other people what they should be thinking or feeling about something or they tell you that it's wrong to feel the way you do about something.

This is a kind of bullying. If someone tries to bully you in this way, you can be your own best friend and stick up for yourself — after all, who can possibly know more about how you feel about something than you do?

Your feelings are yours — no one can make you feel something. If you feel glad or if you feel depressed, that's how you feel.

Of course it may not always be appropriate to say out loud what you are feeling — it's not a good idea for example to tell your head teacher that she annoys you — if that's the case, keep it tactfully to yourself!

MIXED FEELINGS

Sometimes it can be confusing to work out your feelings because you have more than one at a time. This is quite normal:

Suprise, Pleasure

Martin feels surprised to be chosen to sing the solo at the school concert and at the same time he feels pleased.

Sometimes, many different feelings come one after the other:

31

Pleasure, Admiration, Humiliation, Rage
Stephen feels pleased with his new jersey so he puts it on and stands in front of the mirror to admire himself. Suddenly he notices that his brother is looking at him through the window and laughing at him. Stephen feels humiliated that his pleasure in his appearance is being ridiculed. To deal with this painful feeling, he feels rage — how dare Jonathan sneak up on him like that and poke fun!

TALKING ABOUT FEELINGS

Feelings are so much part of our lives that you might expect everyone to be good at talking about them. Sadly, this isn't so. Some people (including lots of adults) are uncomfortable talking about their own feelings and uneasy when they hear other people talking about theirs.

Some people think it's a sign of weakness to talk about feelings. They couldn't be more wrong. In fact, it takes a lot of courage and strength to keep in touch with your feelings and to be able to listen and understand when other people talk about theirs.

Of course, this doesn't mean that you should talk about your feelings to just anyone. You want to be sure that what you are saying will be heard and thought about by someone trustworthy who cares about you. If your parents or the other adults in your life aren't good at talking about feelings, look out for someone who is - perhaps your sister or brother, a friend or your teacher.

GOOD WAYS TO TALK ABOUT FEELINGS
If you say to someone:

* "I'm excited about the party tonight" or
* "I am angry with you for not thanking me for doing that" or
* "I think this TV programme stinks"

you are not hurting that person. You are letting her or him know about your feelings.

If someone tells you:

* "I feel lonely" or
* "I am sad my mum is ill" or
* "I think I'd like to be your friend"

they are letting you know more about them. These are good ways of talking about feelings because they start by saying "I am", "I feel" and "I think".

If you say to someone:

* "You are stupid"

you are talking about them in a bad way.
If you say instead:

* "I think it was stupid of you to run across the road"

you are letting them know how you feel about one thing in particular they did, not telling them that they are a stupid person.

Thinking About Your Feelings

As I've said before, some people would like to be able to control other people's feelings and "make" them feel a particular way about something. But this is just not possible. No one can "make" you feel grateful or pleased or sad or angry or bored or anxious or whatever. Your feelings are not something that can be controlled by other people.

In fact, the only person who really knows and can think about your feelings is you.

As you know, the things we do are linked to the way we feel.

Tom is upset so he cries
Helen is angry with her brother so she slams the door.

But we also control the things we choose to do - you can try not to cry when you are upset or choose not to slam the door when you are angry.

WHEN YOUR FEELINGS GET YOU DOWN
If your feelings are getting you down, you can choose to think about them and see if you can change your response to them. You can turn things around and change them in this way because you are responsible for your feelings. (Of course this doesn't mean that it is wrong to feel sad or angry or jealous or depressed — all these feelings are quite normal and everyone has them.)

James has been given a new bike. He is so excited
that he immediately cycles round to his friend Tony's
house to show him. When he gets there he finds Tony

engrossed in a television show. James has to sit and wait for it to finish before Tony will come out and look at the new bike. James feels disappointed and hurt. James can think about these feelings and he can choose:

1. to think: "If Tony were really my friend, he'd have turned off this stupid programme and come out at once to look at the bike" or

2. to think: "This will soon be over. Just because Tony wants to see the end bit doesn't mean he doesn't want to see my bike."

Mark would like to be in the school football team. He practises hard at weekends and does his best at the trials. He doesn't get chosen.

Mark can think about his feelings of disappointment and he can choose:

1. to feel angry with the teacher for not choosing him and humiliated that all the effort he has made has not been recognised or

2. to feel angry with himself and tell himself "You're obviously hopeless" or

3. to tell himself, "It's very disappointing not to get on

the team but I trained hard and did my best and no one can do more than that. That's OK."

Amy's Gran is ill and there is talk that she may have to go into hospital for an operation. Then Amy's friend Robert tells her that his grandmother has just died. Amy is very worried. She wonders if her Gran is dying but no one has told her the truth.

Amy can think about her feelings of fear and sadness. She can choose:

1. to keep them to herself or

2. to talk to her parents about them and find out the real situation. Perhaps Amy's Gran is not dying. If she is dying, then it will help Amy and her parents if they can talk about it together and share their feelings.

(If someone you love has to go away or if that person is hurt or dies, you will feel full of pain and grief. If you want to cry, that's OK. Crying is a good thing to do — it's good to show your feelings.)

Being Responsible for Your Behaviour

We are all, adults and children, responsible for the way we behave.

Don't Pick on Me

This may seem an odd thing to say in a book addressed to children and young people who are constantly being told how to behave, what to do and what not to do, by all kinds of adults — parents, teachers, park keepers, police officers etc etc.

In fact, none of us — adults or children — can control every bit of our lives and make things happen the way we want them to, however hard we try:

Jackie auditions for the star part in the school play but someone else is picked for it. She tried her hardest to get the part but she can't make the drama teacher decide to give it to her.

Kenneth plans to hang out the washing but then it starts to pour with rain. He can't control the weather, much as he'd like it to be a sunny day so that his best jeans will dry in time for an outing.

But even though Kenneth can't control the weather and Jackie can't control the drama teacher, they can control how they behave in these situations:

Jackie could feel depressed and upset and decide that she'll never try for a part in a play again. Alternatively, Jackie could decide to feel pleased that she had a go and tried her hardest even if it didn't work out; now she'll audition for one of the smaller parts.

Kenneth could feel fed up but decide to make the best of
it and look for another pair of trousers to wear.
Alternatively, Kenneth could choose not to help himself
and allow his feelings of upset to ruin his day completely;
he could refuse to go on the outing at all.

39

MISUSING THE IDEA OF BEING RESPONSIBLE
Sometimes people misuse the idea of being responsible
for their behaviour or they pretend that someone else
"made" them do something.

*Thomas is taking his little sister Susan to the park
while their mum is out. "Mum said we could go on the
swings or feed the ducks," says Susan. "I want to feed
the ducks." "Mum said I was responsible," says
Thomas, "and I want to go on the swings."*

Thomas is using the idea of being responsible for looking
after Susan as an excuse for getting his own way. Susan
is too young to understand that he is being unfair.

*Wendy and Nancy are playing chess in Wendy's
house. Nancy wins two games in a row and Wendy
doesn't like being beaten. They start a third game and
soon it's clear that Nancy will win this one too.
Wendy suddenly tips up the chess board so all the
pieces fall on the floor. "Why did you spoil the
game?" asks Nancy. "You made me do it!" shouts
Wendy. "You kept on winning. It's your fault!"*

Of course Nancy didn't "make" Wendy spoil the game.
Wendy chose to spoil the game all on her own — Wendy
is entirely responsible for her own behaviour.

Michael's parents don't allow him to ride his bike in town as they think the traffic is too dangerous. Michael's friend Phyllis wants him to cycle into town with her to look at new trainers: "Your parents will never know," she says. But Michael's mother catches sight of them as she drives through town and there is trouble for Michael. "You know you're not allowed to ride your bike in town," says Mum, "so why did you do it?" "Phyllis made me go with her," says Michael. "It's not my fault."

Sometimes someone persuades us to do something we're not sure about and we allow ourselves to be persuaded. Michael allowed himself to be persuaded by Phyllis but Phyllis did not "make" Michael ride his bike in town — Michael is responsible for his own behaviour.

Of course lots of adults are also confused about responsibility for their own behaviour:

When Mohan and Laxsmi's father arrives home from work, he finds them quarrelling and fighting over which TV programme to watch. Straight away, he tells their mother that he is going out again and he'll be back later when things have calmed down. Their mother is furious with them and shouts: "You've made your father, who is tired after a hard day at work, go out again before he's eaten his dinner!"

In fact, Mohan and Laxsmi's mother is wrong — the

41

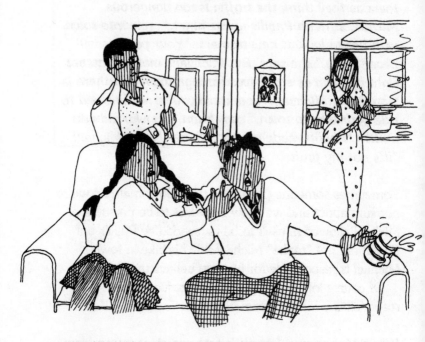

children didn't "make" their father leave. His decision to leave was his responsibility. He could have chosen to stay and asked the children to quieten down.

Whenever adults (or other children) tell you:

"You made me do that"

say to yourself: "I didn't make that person do anything. Other people are responsible for their own behaviour. I am only responsible for my behaviour." This is an important way to stick up for yourself.

42

Of course, if a bully or a gang forces you to do something against your will or an adult misuses her/his authority to make you do something wrong or something that makes you feel uncomfortable, you are not responsible because you are in situation that you cannot control however much you want to. Try to look after yourself as best you can (run off if possible) and tell a trustworthy adult as soon as you can.

Using Your Inner Power

You have power inside you that you may not even know about. You can learn to use this inner power to stick up for yourself.

* If you learn to stick up for yourself, then other people cannot bully you.

* If you learn to stick up for yourself, you won't need to try to control other people by bullying and frightening them.

You may be thinking that it's a bit silly to tell children that they have power. After all, when you are a child you have to do what adults tell you to do. It's very clear that they have power over you.

43

ROLE POWER

It's true that adults, parents and teachers, for example, have power over you. These people can tell you when to go to bed, what medicine to take, what to wear, decide how much pocket money you can have, when you may talk to your friends, etc etc. It can seem as though you have no power at all.

The kind of power that these adults have over you is role power — the kind of power that is part of the job of being a parent or being a teacher.

There are lots of people in society with role power:

* the Prime Minister
* nurses
* traffic wardens
* police officers
* lifeguards
* park keepers
* lollipop men/women

and so on. These people have role power over other adults as well as over children; a park keeper might tell you not to drop litter and tell an adult not to let their dog off the lead.

You may have some role power yourself — perhaps you're:

* captain of the swimming team

44

* head choir boy/girl
* a babysitter.

Janine is a babysitter for a two-year-old and a three-year-old. Her role as babysitter gives her the power to tell them that it's potty time or that they mustn't pull the cat's tail or stick their fingers into electric sockets.

The people with role power who manage that power best, are those who gives choices when that's possible:

Raymond is in charge of a Scout team which has organised a barbecue for the rest of the company on a camping trip. Now the clearing up has to be done. "Shall we do it now or after the sing-song?" Raymond asks. "Oh, let's get it over with!" the team decide.

Raymond has used his role power but made his team feel powerful by giving them a choice.

Of course you don't have to like or agree with everything that people with role power over you make you do. It's sometimes possible to get them to change things — you might succeed, for example, in getting your parents to agree that you can now go to bed half an hour later. It's not very likely that you'd manage to persuade your teacher to allow you to smoke in class for instance.

Some battles are worth fighting and some aren't — often it's not worth fighting people with role power over you even if it's frustrating that they have it.

Of course, this isn't so if that person is misusing their role power. If an adult with role power over you tries to get you to do something that feels uncomfortable or wrong, then don't do it! Find an adult you trust, and tell her/him what happened.

INNER POWER

The power that you can have now and which depends entirely on you, is personal, inner power. If you spend your energy building up this inner power, you will be sticking up for yourself.

You can have inner power even though lots of people have role power over you.

Good Ways to Help Yourself Have Inner Power

One good way to build up your inner power is to remind yourself that you're great as you are. You don't have to:

* pretend to be something you're not
* behave like someone else
* dress like someone else.

Relax, and just be you!

Here are some wrong ideas that might get in the way of the inner power that allows you to be glad to be you. It's all too easy to spend a lot of time worrying about them. Why not just let them go instead?

THINGS TO LET GO

* Let go of the idea that to be liked you have to be like everyone else and fit in with what they want you to do. If you spend your time trying to do this, there'll be no time left to be yourself ...

* Let go of the idea that everyone has to like you. A bus conductor doesn't have to like you to give you a ticket; your dentist doesn't have to like you to fill a hole in your tooth.

* Let go of the idea that if someone doesn't like you, there must be something wrong with you (you've said the wrong thing; you're not wearing the right clothes; you must be awful to be with). Stick up for yourself and start looking at it this way; if someone doesn't like you, it's their problem not yours.

* Let go of the idea that the people you like have to do what you are doing and like what you like all the time. Your friend can go and play football while you paint a picture and still be your friend; your friend can like a different TV programme from you and still be your friend; your friend can enjoy being with other friends and still be your friend. Allow your friends and the people you love to be different from you and to go off and do what's important to them.

47

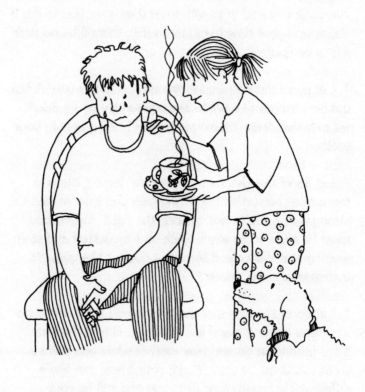

* Let go of the idea that some people are always strong, tough and brave and able to cope and some people are always weak, soft and afraid and in need of help. In fact, we can all be strong or weak, afraid or tough. Sometimes it's nice to be strong and help other people and sometimes it's nice to cry and want to be looked after. You can have both.

* Let go of the idea that if your family really loved you, if your friends were truly your friends, they would know what you want without you having to tell them. Remember that the people who love you, your family and best friends etc, however well they know you, are not mind-readers — they cannot know what you are thinking or hoping. Let them know. Tell them what you want — otherwise you could be waiting around in vain for a long, long time ...

* Let go of the idea that it's shameful to have needs and wants. It's not only not shameful, it's normal. Asking for what you want won't always get you what you want (a chance to try your friend's new racing bike; a trip to Disneyland; a party on your birthday; a hug from your dad). Not asking will get you nowhere.

Allow Yourself to Be You!

Sometimes people are bullied because the bullies think they are "different" in some way. (The idea of people being different is something that frightens some bullies.)

But we are all different from each other. Each one of

us, including you, is rare, individual, beautiful, special —
in fact, absolutely unique. So, it's OK to be different. It's
human to be different.

Part of being human and different is allowing yourself:

* to do what you want to do because you want to do it.

As long as you don't hurt yourself or hurt anyone else or
make them feel bad or break a family or school rule,
doing what you want to do is OK. You don't always have
to have a reason for everything or explain everything you
do. If you feel like going out in the rain so that you can
feel the wetness on your face, then do it.

* to change your mind.

As you get older and become interested in new things
and find out more about other things, you'll want to
branch out in all kinds of ways. Allow yourself to change
your mind — you can decide to be a brain surgeon rather
than a pop star; you can change your favourite food from
pizza to chips; you can change your favourite book from
The Tale of Peter Rabbit to *Lord of the Flies* and you
can decide to like yourself instead of not liking yourself.

* to make mistakes.

There's no one in the world who doesn't make mistakes.
When you're learning something new, you're sure to

make lots of them — but don't give up, just keep trying!
(Remember, if you got everything right the first time you
tried it, many teachers would be out of a job.)

Sometimes you feel bad about making some kinds of
mistakes — like forgetting to send a birthday card or
breaking something or not doing something you
promised to do. When this happens, the important thing
is to try and mend the mistake (why not send that card,
even if it's now a bit late). If that's not possible,
apologise. Think of mistakes as a way of learning how to
do things better (don't use them as excuses!).

Don't Lose Your Inner Power!

When you admire someone, you care very much about
what they think of you. You tend to look up to them and
perhaps behave in a way that you think will please them.
You might even copy the way they behave. This is not
necessarily bad — we can learn a lot by observing people
we admire and seeing if the way that they do things
works for us.

But in this kind of situation, it's easy to lose some of
our inner power to the person or people we admire.

It's important, too, not to get too starry-eyed about
people you admire; at first it may seem as if they have all
the answers. In fact, the only person who really knows
what is best for you, is you.

51

Don't Pick on Me

Mark thinks Peter and Robert are great; he'd really like to be their friend. Mark gets his mum to buy him the kind of sweatshirt and trainers that Peter and Robert have and he starts going to computer club after school because they go. When he finds out they like skateboarding, he starts getting into this too.

Perhaps Mark will make friends with Peter and Robert. Perhaps then he'll relax and do things because they please him, not because he wants to please other people.

Joanna has a riding lesson every weekend at a local stables. One day, Belinda, who owns her own horse and competes in dressage events, starts chatting to her. "You can have a ride on O'Keefe next week if you want to," she says. Joanna is so excited that Belinda has noticed her and been friendly that she offers to stay late and help her muck out.

This may be the start of a good friendship and it may not. Perhaps Belinda is a kind, friendly person who will find it fun to help Joanna learn more about riding. But what if she isn't? What if Joanna turns up next week for her ride on O'Keefe and Belinda is impatient and sneers at the way Joanna rides?

How do you judge whether things are going well or badly for you when you are with someone you admire?

Even if the person you admire is older than you or better than you at doing something, in a good friendship each person respects the other.

How can you tell if this is so?

Listen to your feelings — they will tell you.

If you feel:

* comfortable
* relaxed
* respected as a person
* welcome for just being you

and you're enjoying yourself, then good. It's right for you.

If you feel:

* uneasy
* anxious
* uncomfortable
* put-down

then it's not right for you. Don't stay in situations or go on seeing people who make you feel bad.

Sometimes you'll find that you get along fine with someone most of the time — but then they do something which leaves you feeling powerless and as though there is something wrong with you.

Juliet and Liz like to go to the shopping centre in town on Saturdays to look round and to have a coke. But one day Juliet doesn't turn up at the bus stop to meet Liz as agreed. Liz waits and waits and then goes round to Juliet's house to find her. "Oh, I can't make it today," Juliet says casually, "you don't mind, do you?" Liz does mind. She feels angry and humiliated. She wonders if Juliet didn't come because she doesn't really like her.

This is a horrible feeling for Liz to have. She has to put up with the disappointment of Juliet not turning up and then the worry that it might be because there's something wrong with her. What can she do to get rid of this awful bullying feeling?

Liz is losing her power in this relationship to Juliet. That's why she's feeling so powerless. Liz can't make Juliet turn up at the bus stop but there are steps she can take. She can:

1. tell Juliet how inconsiderate she has been.

2. arrange to call for Juliet at her house instead of hanging about at the bus stop. If she still wants to see her, that is.

3. invite someone else to go to the shopping centre with her instead in the future.

4. be realistic about how reliable Juliet is. Liz may still want to have Juliet as a friend but she can take care not to put herself in a situation where she is reliant on Juliet to turn up.

5. think to herself: "Juliet is a fool to miss out on an afternoon with me. Her loss!"

If Liz does these things she will take back the power she lost to Juliet. In the future, if people let her down, Liz can say to herself: "When people don't stick to arrangements, it's usually because something has happened, like an accident. If it's because they couldn't be bothered, more fool them to miss out on being with me." By doing this, Liz will be slamming the door shut on her own bullying feelings that make her feel bad.

Inner Power For Ever

Now you know a lot about inner power and you can begin to build up your inner power and use it. When you have inner power, you are in charge of yourself.

You can stick up for yourself because you know that:

* No one can "make" you feel something (whether it's glad or sad). You and you alone are responsible for your feelings.

* No one can "make" you do things you shouldn't have done (as in "you made me do it"). You and you alone are responsible for your behaviour.

* You can choose to feel good about yourself even when things don't go right.

* You are learning to make choices that are good for you.

* You can recognise your feelings. You know that it's good to have all of them (the angry, shy, ashamed and frightened ones as well as the excited, glad, joyous ones)

because that's what makes you a complete person.

* Your needs are important. You know what they are and you can try to get them met.

57

Don't Pick on Me

* You can choose not to be powerless in your relationships with people by holding on to your inner power. You can begin to make friends with people with whom you have equal power.

Chapter Three

HAPPINESS WORK-OUTS: HELP YOURSELF TO FEEL GOOD

HAPPINESS WORK-OUTS:
HELP YOURSELF TO FEEL GOOD

Be a good friend to yourself by practising these exercises. They will help to remind you of all the good things about you.

Happiness Work-Out No.1:
When You Feel Lonely or Sad

When you feel lonely or sad, give yourself a treat: do something nice for yourself that you enjoy. It doesn't have to be something that costs money or something very complicated to organise. You could:

* stroke a friendly cat
* have a long, hot bath
* watch a sunset
* look in your favourite shop window
* draw a picture
* watch your favourite comedy show on TV

Don't Pick on Me

Start a list of things like these that you enjoy. When you enjoy something new, add it to your list so that it's not forgotten. And don't just keep these nice things for when you're feeling lonely or sad — look at your list from time to time and if you enjoyed, say, going to the park and watching the ducks swimming about, find time to do it again.

Happiness Work-Out No.2: Nice Things About You

Being a good friend to yourself means that you can say nice things to yourself about you. You can also remind yourself of all the things that you can do.

Make two lists: one of nice things about you and one of the things that you can do. You can include things like "I'm a good swimmer" even if you're not the best swimmer in your school (you don't have to be a champion at things to be able to include them). These are your personal lists and your personal good things about you.

You might include things like:

Nice Things I Know About Me
* I'm a good friend to have
* I like animals
* I have beautiful eyelashes
* I'm a good listener

Things I Can Do
* I'm good at catching
* I know a lot about space travel
* I'm a good speller
* I've got a good memory

When something happens that makes you think "Why would anyone like me anyway?" or "I messed that up. I can't get anything right," remember all the things listed under "Nice Things I Know About Me" and "Things I Can Do" and be kinder to yourself. The nice things that you have listed will help you to stick up for yourself with yourself and be less critical.

Happiness Work-Out No.3: Look After Yourself

Get into the habit of doing something good for your body and something good for your brain everyday. It could be:

Body
* Going swimming
* Eating some fruit
* Washing your hair
* Cutting your toenails

Brain
* Following a story on the news
* Solving a puzzle
* Learning a song
* Browsing in the library.

Happiness Work-Out No.4:
The Praise Box

Whenever someone says something nice to you about you or praises something you have done, write it down and store it away in your praise box. Open your praise box every so often and remind yourself of all these nice things that have been said by all these different people.

Happiness Work-Out No.5:
The Difference Game

Play this game with a friend or someone in your family. Sit down together and take it in turns to:

1. Tell each other all the things that make you different from each other.

2. Tell each other all the things you like about each other.

Happiness Work-Out No.6:
The Letting Go Game

Is your stomach tight? Are your fists clenched? Are your nails bitten? Does your chest feel empty and hurting? Do you have a headache? Are your teeth clenched? Are your

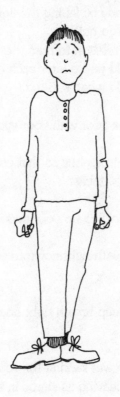

shoulders tight and high instead of loose and relaxed?

When your body feels clenched and tight in ways like this, it is showing you that you are anxious or frightened or sad or hurting. Listen to what your body is telling you and look after these feelings.

Your body talks to you all the time and lets you know when things are going well for you and when they're not. Keep in touch with your body and listen to its messages. Look after your body by letting the tightness or emptiness or pain go out of it.

Ask a friend or relation to read these directions to you slowly. S/he should pause after each one and give you plenty of time to do what is asked.

1. Lie down on the floor with your eyes closed.

2. Tuck your chin in slightly so that your spine and neck feel long and comfortable.

3. Feel the floor holding up your body.

4. Take a deep breath right down to your tummy. Let it out slowly.

5. Take another deep breath right down to your tummy. Let it out slowly.

6. Imagine lying in wet sand at the seaside. Imagine each part of your body leaving its shape in the sand.

7. Slowly relax each bit of you into the sand starting with your head and working down to your toes. Let all the tightness run out of you.

8. Lie quietly for a few moments breathing deeply.

9. When you're ready, open your eyes and sit up slowly.

Chapter Four

SELF-PROTECTION STRATEGIES

Chapter Four

SELF-PROTECTION STRATEGIES

Physical Bullying

As you get older, you will probably find that you prefer to settle arguments by discussion rather than by punching the person you are having an argument with. Learning to use words rather than fists is part of growing up.

Unfortunately, some people go on using physical aggression — punching, hitting, slapping, hair pulling, fighting — as a means of bullying other people and trying to get their own way. Such bullies almost always pick on people to fight or beat up who are smaller or weaker than they are or less good at fighting. Because these bullies use physical violence a lot to get their own way, they are often very good fighters.

If you're not good at fighting or you don't want to fight, the most sensible thing you can do when faced with a bully who is threatening you physically is to follow the advice of the old saying:

Run, run, run away,
Live to fight another day.

Don't Pick on Me

(Hopefully, you'll find a way so that you don't have to fight "another day" either. Who needs it?)

THE DAVID AND GOLIATH MYTH
Perhaps you know the Bible story about David and Goliath? David the shepherd boy goes out to fight the champion of the Philistines, a huge man called Goliath who is armed with a shield and a spear and covered with armour. Tiny David has nothing but his shepherd's staff, a sling and five pebbles and yet he succeeds in killing Goliath. (Of course, he has God on his side ...)

There are lots of stories like this about the small and weak defeating the big and powerful in a fight. Unfortunately, in almost all fights in playgrounds and elsewhere, it is the small, the weak and those who aren't good fighters or who don't want to fight who get pulverised by the big, powerful bullies.

Trying Not to Fight

If you can't run away or avoid the bullies who want to fight you or beat you up, some of these tactics may be useful:

* Try to bluff your way out, eg, by pretending that a teacher is waiting for you or that your dad is on his way to pick you up.

* Walk away if you can. A fight takes two people — if you refuse to fight, this can stop the bully from hurting you. This can be a hard thing to do because it can appear that the bully has won — perhaps that you have accepted the bully's insults. If your friends are watching, you might feel honour bound to stand there and let yourself be beaten up in case they think you are a coward. But remember, if you manage to walk away without a fight taking place, you will have succeeded in leaving without you being physically hurt and without you having to hurt anyone else. It takes great strength and

courage to turn your back on the jeers and taunts and walk away.

* Lots of fights start with a person who decides that they have been insulted:

"What did you call me?"
"Who do you think you're staring at?"
"Say that again, if you dare!"
etc. etc. etc.

Bullies who enjoy fights like to seek out reasons to feel insulted on purpose — it gives them an excuse to beat someone up!

This kind of fight often happens in playgrounds and everyone rushes to watch. Because there is an audience, a bully is not likely to back down easily. In an ideal world, a good friend of the person who is being picked on would run off to find a teacher to stop the fight developing. (But this isn't always an ideal world.)

If you find yourself being picked on by a bully who is trying to start a fight, try to keep thinking and stay cool even if you are being insulted. Try not to be drawn into insulting the bully back.

If you can, agree with the bully. For example, if the bully calls you "four eyes" because you wear glasses and accuses you of being afraid to fight, you can agree that, yes, you do wear glasses and, yes, you don't like to fight. Agreeing to things like these doesn't mean you are a coward — they are facts and nothing to be ashamed of.

If the bully insults you in abusive ways or says horrible things that aren't true, disagree but try to do it in a calm way. You could simply say, for example, "That is not true."

What bullies always want is to get a reaction from the people they bully — they want you to get angry or to look scared. If you can manage not to react to the insults you might manage to get away without being beaten up or having to fight.

* Stand up to a bully. To try this, you have to choose your moment - preferably one when there's no one else about to see what's going on. (If there are other people around, the bully may feel that s/he can't be seen to back down.) Try to look confident and relaxed and say something direct like, "You may not like me, but I want you to know that I'm not going to let you bully me/hurt me/take my things any more!" Of course this may not work, but if you sense that it might, it's worth a try. Bullies expect the people they bully to be afraid, so if you surprise them by standing up to them, they might just back down.

* Talk your way out. If you're good at using words, good at verbal arguments, this is worth a try. If you've got a sense of humour too, you might even be able to joke your way out of a tight spot. But take care! Don't let the bullies think that you're laughing at them or that you think they are stupid.

75

* Threaten to tell and tell. Bullies have no right to hurt you. Go for it! Be sure you do tell.

You might think that telling an adult or someone older about bullying is cowardly. This is not so. If someone is trying to hurt you, you have the right to get someone older or someone in authority like your teacher to protect you. Protecting children and young people is part of the job for teachers, playground supervisors and police officers as it is for parents. Not all of them, unfortunately, can be relied on to stop fights in a gentle, wise and tactful way, but when you risk being beaten up, the important thing is to stop the violence quickly before you get hurt.

When It's All Over

If you've been in a threatening situation but managed to get out of it without a fight, you'll need to tell someone you trust what happened and talk it through. Situations of this kind are very frightening. You might also be feeling angry or humiliated that you didn't manage to stop the bullies insulting you or stop them saying untrue or unfair things. Remember that you did well in a tricky situation. It's only in films that the hero gets the bullies to eat their words too.

If you have been beaten up, you'll also need to talk about it with an adult you trust. You'll need to discuss

76

whether you want to make a complaint against the people who hurt you and how to make sure this situation doesn't happen again. You may need to see a doctor. Above all, you'll need time to get your confidence back. Remember, you didn't deserve to be beaten up. It's OK to feel angry about it. It's OK to feel upset about it.

Should You Learn to Fight?

Even if you become a karate black belt, there is no guarantee that you will never be bullied ever again. However, being taught to fight properly will lessen your chances of being bullied. Just the fact that you look more confident will lessen your chances of being picked on.

The best way to learn to fight is to join a self-defence class or a class that teaches one of the martial arts such as karate. Your local library should be able to help you find out what's available in your area.

Classes like these can be a big help in making you feel more confident when you are faced with aggression. They will help you protect yourself and deal with the aggression without being frightened. They should also teach you ways of getting out of threatening situations by non-violent means.

If you are someone who fights in order to get your own way and to bully and control other people, you could also find these classes useful as they will teach you how to use your anger and aggression and fighting skills in more positive ways.

But it is very important to be realistic about what you can achieve by learning self-defence or one of the martial arts. Remember that:

* You will not turn into Wonderwoman or Superman, so you must not start taking silly risks.

* Self-defence and martial arts' techniques need to be practised and kept up or your skills will rust.

* Fighting back physically is just one possible way to handle a situation in which you are being threatened and should be a last resort. Don't forget the other, non-violent options.

Who Started It?

Sometimes someone who is being bullied fights back or perhaps even attacks first in a desperate attempt to stop the bully hurting them again. If a teacher or some other adult who does not know anything about the bullying that has been going on, spots this, s/he might misinterpret the situation and blame the victim for bullying instead of the real bully.

If this happens to you, it is very hard. Try to get your friends or other witnesses to come with you and explain what really happened. Your parents may also be able to help you sort things out.

Of course, teachers and other adults should take care when they investigate incidents of bullying that they are getting the whole story. They should not assume that what they happened to see was an isolated incident. In fact, it might be just one example among very many of bullying taking place.

A school with an effective anti-bullying policy should

aware of this problem and have a way of investigating incidents of bullying thoroughly.

Teasing

Verbal bullying happens when a bully uses words to hurt someone by, eg, name-calling or making them look silly. If you have been bullied in this way, you may find that people say "Oh, it's just a bit of teasing. You should be able to take that. Perhaps you've got no sense of humour!"

In fact, there are important differences between verbal bullying and teasing that you should be clear about.

When you are being teased:

* Someone is making fun of you in a good-humoured way.

* Often the person doing the teasing is someone who knows you well and cares about you, like your mum or your grandad.

* Teasing is not something to be taken seriously — usually you'll find it funny too.

* If you do feel upset by teasing, it's a mild feeling that soon goes away.

* Teasing is a two-way thing — someone who teases will soon get teased and someone who is teased will soon become a teaser.

SCHOOL TEASING
At school lots of people get teased, usually because they are different in some way from the others. This can be hard to take if you're not used to it. People who have been teased a lot at home by sisters and brothers find it easier to cope with because they have had a lot of practice. Try to keep a sense of humour if you can!

If you're finding teasing upsetting, it's a good idea to prepare yourself for it.

If you've got to have braces on your teeth, for example, and tomorrow is the first time you'll have to appear at school with them, why not think about how you might be teased about them and what you can say in reply:

* I've been signed up to star in the next Jaws movie.

* You have to suffer to be beautiful.

* Actually, *your* teeth look like they need braces to me.

* You're just jealous because you don't have any.

Ask your mum or dad or some other caring adult to help you prepare for possible teasing. S/he can pretend to be the teaser and you can try out your replies. This will help to give you confidence. (You might even find, to your surprise, that no one comments on your braces the next day at school.)

The other thing to remember about teasing is that if you don't react, you probably won't get teased. Teasers like the people they tease to react by being amused or upset. If you don't react, they will stop.

Verbal Bullying

* When teasing becomes cruel and causes someone distress, it has slipped over the dividing line between teasing and bullying and become bullying.

* When teasing becomes one-sided and the same person is always at the receiving end, then teasing has become bullying.

* Some of the tactics described to deal with physical bullying will also help with verbal bullying. Often of course, bullies use a mixture of physical and verbal threats.

VERBAL THREATS
If bullies threaten you, the best thing to do is tell a trusted adult what has happened.

Sometimes bullies will try to make you do something or give them something by threatening to tell the world a secret they know about you that you would like kept private. This is called blackmail. The best way to deal with blackmail, if at all possible, is to say, "Tell whoever you like. I don't care!" This takes a lot of courage. (We all have embarrassing secrets.) If you can, talk to a trusted adult about the problem — your secret may not be as embarrassing as you think.

If you are being taunted and jeered at by bullies, it can

be very hard to bear. Turn to Chapter 2 on sticking up for yourself and remind yourself of all the good things about you.

Bullying Yourself

Getting rid of the bully inside you takes a while. Read Chapter Two of this book about sticking up for yourself and enjoy doing the happiness work-outs.

Where Bullying Takes Place

Most cases of bullying take place at school — indeed, one researcher found that one-fifth of children are bullied at some point in their school career. But bullying can also take place going to and from school; some of the most violent cases of bullying have happened at this time when adults are not there to supervise. These incidents can involve children from the same school or from other schools.

When a school anti-bullying policy is drawn up, safety going to and from school must also be considered.

Bullying can also be carried out in the home — by brothers and sisters and by parents. Sometimes children are so used to being treated in a bullying way in their home that they don't even realise that they are being bullied. It is difficult for children brought up in such homes not to believe that hostile and aggressive ways of

84

treating people are normal and acceptable. It is possible that some children who bully others at school do so because they, in turn, are bullied at home.

Bullying at Boarding School

In the past, some people believed that bullying in boarding schools was good for pupils and prepared them for the "real world". Boarding schools had fagging (new pupils had to do chores for older pupils) and even prefects were allowed to beat and punish young pupils.

Unfortunately corporal punishment (being beaten or hit) is still legal in private schools in the UK, many of which are boarding schools. It is hard to believe that a school which allows corporal punishment can be a school which takes seriously the prevention of bullying. When bullies see teachers enforcing their own way by hitting or beating people smaller than themselves who are in their power, it does not set the bullies a good example of how they might behave better towards other people.

People at boarding school are usually more closely supervised by teachers and other staff than children at day schools. This can sometimes help to stop bullying taking place.

On the other hand, if bullying is taking place, it can be very difficult for the victims of bullying to escape because there is nowhere to escape to — no safe place where the bullies cannot find them. Sometimes boarding school pupils cannot even feel safe at night if there are bullies in their dormitory. Boarding school children have reported quite serious assaults taking place in dormitories at night and at the weekends, sometimes carried out by older children who are monitors or prefects.

Another problem faced by many people at boarding school is that they cannot make phone calls or can only make them at particular times, or they cannot make phone calls in a private place where they cannot be overheard. As a result, they cannot call their parents or a helpline for advice. If you are in this difficult and frightening situation, try to find a sympathetic teacher to talk to. If this is not possible, perhaps you can write to your parents or Childline about what is going on.

Group Bullying

When bullying is done by a group of bullies rather than by one individual, it can be particularly difficult for the victim of the bullying to deal with it because they will experience rejection and hurt by a whole group of hostile people rather than by just one person. It's easy for a group of bullies to make even the most confident person feel isolated, friendless, weak, lonely and powerless; you may even begin to wonder if there isn't, after all, something wrong with you. (Answer: No!) This can be the hardest kind of bullying to deal with, especially if it goes on for any length of time. If this is happening to you, don't try to cope with it on your own — no one could. Try to find a trustworthy adult to tell.

Some bullies seek out situations where they can have an audience because they enjoy being surrounded by admirers and supporters and having their every word listened to with attention. If they use sarcasm or wit to bully the victim and/or some physical violence, they like an appreciative crowd. In this situation, the level of cruelty and violence used by the bully or bullies to torment the victim can increase just because there is an audience to play to.

In this gang or group situation, those taking part in these cruel and hurtful activities may not feel personal responsibility. This is because so many others are also taking part and "sharing" the blame. In fact, even though they are not acting alone, each and every one of the bullies taking part in group bullying is personally responsible for what takes place.

Many children who are part of a group of bullies would not behave in this way if they were on their own. If this is happening to you, you should be aware that the desire to be part of a group or gang can sometimes lead you into saying or doing cruel and evil things that you would not dream of saying or doing if you were on your own.

Being different to everyone else in the gang or refusing to do something everyone else is doing can be difficult and painful and make you afraid that you will lose your friends. Sometimes a group or gang will use jeers and threats to make you go along with what they want to do ("You're chicken!" "Why not run home to Mummy?" etc).

When you go along with something that you wouldn't do as an individual you are avoiding taking responsibility for your actions. You pretend to yourself that what is happening isn't your fault, you didn't start it.

The fact is, however, that your very presence may be encouraging the bully or bullies by giving them an audience.

These group/gang situations are hard to handle but it is always possible that if you are uncomfortable or shocked about something the group/gang is doing then some of the others may be too — perhaps they are also too scared to say so. You could try appealing to the nicer people to support you in not taking part or stopping what is being done. If the situation is really out of hand you should not take part, saying why if you can. You should also try to leave or call for help.

You need to be aware of the dangers of group/gang psychology so that you can recognise it and avoid becoming a victim of it. As a member of a group or gang you must also be able to avoid being pressurised into going along with something that you will later regret and feel ashamed about.

Telling About Bullying

The rule that you should never tell about bullying is a rule invented by bullies for their own benefit. Obviously, it makes things very convenient for them. Not only can they bully in peace but a victim of their bullying cannot complain about it without being called a "grass", a "telltale", a "crybaby" or a "wimp".

Some adults are confused about whether telling about bullying is a good thing or a bad thing. Many of them were taught as children that bullying is "good for you" (it "toughens you up"); or that it's something you learn to cope with as you get older; or that there's something dishonourable or humiliating in asking for help when you're being bullied — you ought to be able to deal with it yourself. This idea (that bullying is something you should be able to cope with on your own) is very widespread. The people who work on phone helplines report fewer calls from older children even though people in this age group are still bullied — perhaps they are embarrassed to ask for help, feeling that they should be able to cope on their own.

Some people do find ways to cope on their own but some can't. Sometimes the bullying is so severe that no one could deal with it on their own. Remember, even adults are bullied! There is never anything wrong with asking for help. (In fact it takes great courage and strength to do it.)

ASKING FOR HELP

The real problems with asking an adult for help when you are bullied are:

* whether that adult will be willing to help.

When Janine told her Mum about being taunted and pushed around in the playground her mum told her it would soon stop. If it was still going on next term she would do something about it.

It can make you feel quite despairing to have finally plucked up the courage to tell an adult about being bullied, only to find that they cannot or will not help. You need to find another adult who may find it easier to understand and help. You could also phone one of the helplines (see below).

* whether the adult you've told will handle the situation tactfully and sensibly.

When Theresa's headteacher talked in assembly about bullying, she did it in such a way that it was obvious to the bullies that Theresa had "told". From then on, Theresa was bullied worse than before.

When Andrew told his dad about the boys who threw his sports equipment around the changing room and tore his shirt, Dad went straight round to school the next day and threatened to punch the bullies. Andrew was jeered at and taunted for the rest of the term.

HOW ADULTS SHOULD DEAL WITH BULLYING

If you are being bullied you usually want the adult you tell to do three things:

1. Stop the bullying.

2. Stop the bullying in such a way that neither the bully nor anyone else knows that you have told.

3. Treat the bully firmly but with understanding. Often you will be afraid that if the bully suffers because you have told, it will rebound on you.

Sometimes even the most sensible, sensitive and experienced adult is not able to manage all three things. Sometimes it's inevitable that a bully gets to know that you have told. (In this case, the adult should work out in advance how to handle things so you don't get tormented more or isolated by your classmates.) If you tell your mum or dad, they will have to work out with the school how best to proceed.

These days many more adults, particularly teachers, are aware of bullying and the need to handle it sensitively and tactfully. In a study done of a Bullying Helpline (no longer available) it was found that nearly three-quarters of the children who had asked for adult help found that it had positive effects.

When bullying occurs, adult help is almost always needed to deal with it, and that adult help can be effective if properly carried out.

Your parents and teachers may find the end section of this book which lists organisations involved with bullying helpful — many offer advice and information on strategies to deal with bullying.

Good Ways to Tell Tales

* Remember that not telling helps the bullies go on bullying — and you are almost certainly not the only person who is or will be bullied by them. By telling you will be helping to create an atmosphere where people can feel safe and confident that they will be well treated instead of feeling frightened and insecure because they might be bullied.

* Tell with someone if you can — take a friend or a witness or your mum or dad with you. It's good to have someone there for you.

* Don't suffer bullying for a long time. Perhaps you want to try and stop it on your own — fine. But if you don't manage, don't let it drag on. Get help. The longer bullying goes on, the harder it will be to put an end to it.

* As a last resort and if your school really won't help

bullying to stop, it may be possible for you to change schools. Discuss this with your mum and dad.

More Sensible Self-Protection Strategies

When there are bullies around, it's sensible to:

1. Stick with your friends whenever you can. Be part of a group.

2. In the playground, keep within sight of a teacher or supervisor.

3. Try not to react to teasing or bullying by showing that you are upset or angry. Try to keep and look calm. Bullies lose interest in bullying people who don't react.

4. Don't show off by wearing expensive jewellery or taking other expensive items into school with you.

5. If bullies take your dinner money or steal something of yours, try not to get into a fight. It's not worth being beaten up for the price of a school dinner. Tell a trusted adult what happened and who was responsible as soon as you can and talk through how you're going to ensure that it doesn't happen again.

6. Practise your replies to things that you may be teased or bullied about (embarrassing initials, unusual name, spectacles, hearing aid, red hair, black skin, freckles, tall, short, plump, etc etc) so that you can give the impression that it doesn't bother you.

Stopping Being a Bully: Sensible Strategies

If you are a bully, it's possible to spend the rest of your life in win/lose situations. That is you "win" when you bully someone and they lose. But do you really win? You are not going to be offered real friendship and respect by people you bully or by people who see you bully. They can only fear you. You don't need to lead your life in this sad way; you can change your behaviour. Here are some ideas that may be helpful:

1. Observe how relaxed, confident, happy people get on together without needing to bully or control each other. Are there ways of doing things here you can learn from?

2. Are you a bully because you are bullied at home — by your parents or by older brothers or sisters? If this is so, you know how painful it is to be bullied. Think of how you would like to be treated and start trying to treat yourself and other people in these good ways.

3. Why not put your physical energies and aggression into sport? It's OK to win there by beating other people so long as you stick to the rules of the game. Watch the athletes you admire on television and find out if you could train for that sport.

4. Think about the pain that verbal bullying can cause — as much if not more than physical bullying. (Sometimes people just don't realise how much words can hurt and that they are being bullies.)

5. Why not be a leader but without trying to dominate

and control other people? Good leaders are people who look after their team or group, making sure everyone is treated fairly and everyone's point of view is heard. Perhaps joining an outward bound course, Guides or Scouts is something that might channel and develop your leadership skills?

6. Think about the heroes you admire in films, books or television. Are they people like Rambo who settle arguments by punching, shooting and knifing "enemies"? If so, try to think of other heroes who win through by using other kinds of strength.

7. What is it about the people that you bully that irritates you? You might not realise, say, that Peter always looks timid because you frighten him; Yvonne is clumsy because she was born with a defect of the hips that cannot be cured; Jane would love to have nice clothes like the other girls in class but her family cannot afford them. And so forth. Try to see other people as whole people and as different from you as you are different from them.

8. Do you enjoy bullying because you enjoy showing off in front of an audience? It's possible to get that kind of enjoyment without hurting other people — for example by acting in a school play or being good at sports. Why not try these instead?

An Anti-Bullying School Policy

If your school really wants to tackle the problem of bullying, it is important not just to deal with it each time it occurs but to have an anti-bullying policy. Children and young people can play an important part in putting such a policy together because it must be tailor-made for their particular school.

These days quite a few schools have anti-bullying policies and these do help to create an atmosphere in which pupils feel safe and confident that if bullying does occur, it will be noticed and dealt with both wisely and speedily.

Of course, such schools cannot guarantee that bullying will never again take place. No school can afford to think that. It's important that every school constantly monitors and checks that it is bully-free.

Here are some ideas that your teachers might find useful in organising an anti-bullying policy for your school:

1. The whole school should be organised in such a way that no one teacher or pupil is left to cope with a bullying problem alone. Everyone who works or studies at the school — the head, the teachers, the caretaker, the dinner ladies, the playground supervisors, the pupils, the governors etc — should all be involved in monitoring and tackling bullying.

98

2. Everyone should be made aware that bullying is not allowed in the school in any form. A statement to this effect should be drawn up and given to every pupil and their parents. The statement should also emphasise the positive role that everyone can play in encouraging caring and responsible attitudes to other people.

3. Pupils and teachers should discuss the layout of the school and its grounds and the routes taken by pupils to and from school. They should identify where bullying takes place (eg the corridors, classrooms when it's wet playtime, the toilets, the school bus) and at what time of day. Proper supervision of these areas should then be organised.

4. Pupils and teachers should discuss which groups of people are more likely to be bullied (eg new first years; people who transfer from other schools) and see whether there are ways they can be helped to feel safe. It might be possible, for example, for older pupils to be given the responsibility of looking after new first years as they settle in — showing them around, taking a friendly interest, being alert to any anxieties or threats of bullying.

5. Large secondary schools can be very frightening places for new pupils. Older pupils could help by preparing maps, notices and signs for them so that they can easily find their way around.

6. Pupils and teachers could organise regular discussions of bullying and issues connected with bullying. This might include studying particular books, plays or videos which treat the issues (see suggested titles list at the end of this book).

Conclusion

Bullying has long been an event that children have had to suffer alone, uncertain as to whether the adults who care for them will listen or help if they manage to tell of their anxiety or suffering.

Now at last, bullying is beginning to be openly discussed, at least in some schools, and many children are beginning to find the support and help they need. For children who bully, the beginnings of an approach that seeks to understand and help change to take place is likewise under way.

Adults also encounter bullies but they at least can call upon unions, counsellors, the police and so forth to help them.

Most children believe strongly in fairness and welcome the introduction of ways of interacting that treat others with care and respect — ways that many aspire to and can achieve.

Further Information

Further Information

QUESTIONS AND ANSWERS

Q.
Bullying is normal. It's always happened and it always will. Shouldn't children just toughen up and deal with it themselves?

A.
Unfortunately bullying is something that happens all too often so, yes, children should learn to deal with it, hopefully with help from sympathetic adults. On the other hand, it is not "normal" for people — adults or children — to live in an atmosphere of fear and insecurity, which is what happens when bullying is allowed to go on.

Some children do manage to deal with bullying on their own without being too hurt by it — generally they are people with high self-esteem (lots of "inner power") who do not allow bullying to influence how they see themselves. Other children whose self-esteem is more fragile, find bullying very distressing and they lose confidence in themselves. Sometimes bullying can be so long term or so vicious that even the most confident person would find it impossible to deal with on their own.

People who have been bullied can suffer from the effects even in later life, finding it hard to trust other people, hard to form relationships and hard to have any confidence in their own worth. Children who are bullied may become truants, fall behind with their work, suffer from depression and have even, in some cases, committed suicide.

All this amounts to very good reasons for children who are bullied to seek adult help as soon as possible rather than try to deal with it themselves.

Q.
You say that if you are bullied or teased you should try not to let the bullies see how upset you are. Isn't it harmful to bottle up your feelings like this? And why shouldn't the bullies and teasers know how hurt you are feeling?

A.
Part of growing up is learning when it is appropriate to show your feelings and when it's not. It's not a good idea to show the people who are tormenting you that they are succeeding in upsetting and hurting you, if you can avoid it. Sometimes of course, it's just not possible not to cry or not to look as frightened as you feel. But if you are

able to appear indifferent, this is a good strategy to stop the teasing or bullying. Those people who bully and tease do so to get a reaction from their victim — they want to know that they have succeeded in hurting or upsetting or embarrassing you. If you don't react, they'll stop doing it.

Of course you need to talk about what happened when you were bullied or teased and how painful and hurtful it was, but you should do this with people you trust and know are on your side. After such a horrible experience you need to be with people with whom you feel secure.

Q.
Do child bullies grow up to be adult bullies?

A.
If child bullies are not helped to find other ways of dealing with their aggression or other troubling feelings, it is very possible (although not inevitable) that they will continue to bully and be aggressive in adult life. This is a sad way to live a life.

People sometimes find the idea that bullies deserve understanding hard to take when bullies do such horrible and mean things to others. But it is very important that children who bully get sympathetic adult help so that they can be released from the pain and fear that they express in their bullying behaviour and learn happier ways to get on with other people.

107

Don't Pick on Me

Q.

I am really embarrassed about my middle name (Cynthia) and I haven't told anyone what it is. My friend saw it written in the school register and now she's threatening to tell everyone. I'll die if she tells.

A.

Nobody died from having a middle name they hated. Why not take the wind out of your "friend's" sails by telling everyone about it yourself? You could say something like: "What names don't you like? My worst name is Cynthia and, guess what, that's my middle name. I don't know what my parents could have been thinking of." Don't let people like your "friend" torment you in this way — few personal things are really as embarrassing as they seem. Remember, Winston Churchill's initials were W.C.

Q.

My ears stick out and I get called "jug-ears" at school. I tried growing my hair to hide them but people still make fun of me.

A.

You're in good company — Prince Charles's ears stick out too. Remember that teasers will go on making fun so long as you let them see that you are reacting. Try to imagine that your head is enclosed in a giant bubble.

When you are teased the teasing can't break through the bubble — it just bounces off. Try also to keep a sense of humour — people who can laugh at themselves don't get picked on. On a practical note, it is possible to have sticking-out ears operated on. Why not get advice from your GP about what's available.

Q.
When you advise children to list all the things they are good at and the nice things people have said about them, you're just going to encourage them to be big-headed.

Don't Pick on Me

A.
I wish more children were big-headed, if that means that they are aware of the things they have done well and feel pleased with themselves. In fact, a lot of parents and teachers don't give as much praise and encouragement as children need and deserve. If you listen to the way parents and teachers talk to children, you'll find that most of the time they are telling them what not to do, not praising them for things they have done well.

WHERE TO GET HELP AND ADVICE

When you need help, try to talk to someone you trust —
perhaps your parents or your teacher. If you don't have
anyone you can talk to, contact these organisations.
Many of them are in London but some have branches in
different parts of the country that they can put you in
touch with. London numbers start with 071 or 081.

Helplines

These help and advice phone lines are free (you don't
need a phone card or money, just dial the number) and
open 24 hours:

Childline
0800 1111

NSPCC (National Society for the Prevention of Cruelty to
Children)
0800 800500

111

Don't Pick on Me

RSSPCC (The Royal Scottish Society for the Prevention
of Cruelty to Children)
031 337 8539

The Samaritans
0345 909090
You will find the number of your local branch in the
phone book or you can ask the operator to put you
through directly.

Organisations

Advisory Centre for Education (ACE)
1B Aberdeen Studios
22 Highbury Grove
London N5 2EA
tel: 071 354 8321

Anti-Bullying Campaign
18 Elmgate Gardens
Edgware
Middlesex HA8 9RT
tel: 071 378 1446

Childline
Freepost 1111
London N1 0BR
0800 1111

Children's Legal Centre
20 Compton Terrace
London N1 2UN
071 359 6251

Kidscape
World Trade Centre
Europe House
3rd Floor
London E1 9AA
071 730 3300

Videos

Hands on Bullying
Examples of bullying in a secondary school and what can
be done about it. Available from Tony Jewers
Productions, 4 Greystones Close, Colchester, Essex
CO3 4RQ

My Life as a Bully
Set in a comprehensive school, this video is humorous
and entertaining but also designed to provoke discussion.
Available from Firehouse Productions, 9 Clarendon
Villas, Hove, East Sussex BN3 3RD

Books

1. For Teachers and Parents

Bullies and Victims in Schools
Valerie Besag (Open University Press)
An overview of the research into bullying and methods
used in schools to combat it.

Bullying: A Practical Guide to Coping for Schools
Michele Elliott (Ed) (Longman)

Bullying, The Child's View
Jean La Fontaine (Calouste Gulbenkian Foundation)
An analysis of telephone calls to Childline about bullying.

Bullying: A Positive Response
Delwyn Tattum and Graham Herbert (from Cardiff
Institute of Higher Education)
Advice to parents, teachers and governors.

2. For Children

UNDER FIVES

Willy the Wimp
Anthony Browne (Julia MacRae Books)

Hurrah for Ethelyn
Babette Cole (Heinemann)

SIX TO EIGHT YEAR OLDS

Trouble with the Tucker Twins
Rose Impey (Viking)

No More Bullying!
Rosemary Stones (Dinosaur)

Feeling Happy, Feeling Safe
Michele Elliott (Hodder & Stoughton)

Bullying
Angela Grunsell (Franklin Watts)

The Angel of Nitshill Road
Anne Fine (Methuen)

Burper
Robert Leeson (Heinemann)

EIGHT TO TWELVE YEAR OLDS

Bullies at School
Theresa Breslin (Blackie Snappers)

Don't Pick on Me

The Present Takers
Aidan Chambers (Mammoth)

Bully
Yvonne Coppard (Red Fox)

The Bully
Jan Needle (Hamish Hamilton)

TWELVE YEARS AND UPWARDS

Lord of the Flies
William Golding (Penguin)

INDEX